BOBBY & JACKIE ANGEL
with FR. MIKE SCHMITZ

PRAY, DECIDE _AND_

DON'T WORRY

5 STEPS TO DISCERNING GOD'S WILL

ASCENSION

West Chester, Pennsylvania

Excerpts from the English translation of the *Catechism of the Catholic Church* for use in the United States of America. Copyright © 1994, 1997 United States Catholic Conference, Inc.–Libreria Editrice Vaticana. Used by permission. All rights reserved.

Unless otherwise noted, Scripture passages are from the *Revised Standard Version Bible, Second Catholic Edition.* Copyright © 2006 Division of Christian Education of the National Council of the Churches of Christ in the United States of America. Used by permission. All rights reserved.

Ascension
P.O. Box 1990
West Chester, PA 19380
1-800-376-0520
ascensionpress.com

Cover design: Kathleen Raymundo

Printed in the United States of America
20 21 22 23 6 5 4 3

ISBN 978-1-945179-78-5

This book is dedicated to all young people in love with the Lord who are actively seeking God's plan for their lives.

God is faithful.

CONTENTS

INTRODUCTION

Following the will of God in your life is the most fulfilling thing you will ever do.

When we fall in love with the Lord, everything changes. We have a desire to truly know, follow, and serve him in all that we do.

But *how* we put that love into action can be downright confusing and exhausting. Often there are no instant answers to the questions we ask. Sometimes there are several paths we can take, and there is no clear "right" or "wrong" choice. This can be confusing, difficult, and discouraging. We can grow weary and wonder if the journey to find God's will is worth it. We can question whether finding God's will is truly possible.

Consider the following questions:

Why am I here?

Lord, what do you want me to do?

Why don't I hear anything when I pray?

If I choose wrongly, am I doomed to a life of misery?

What if I never find out?

Why do I feel so much fear?

Lord, why won't you just TELL me your plan already so I can get to work?

If you are asking any of the above questions, know that you are not alone, and this book was written for you. We know that the pace of modern life and the culture we live in does not make it easy to slow down, experience silence, or grow in prayer to be able to hear God's voice. We expect everything to be delivered or downloaded instantly, and we live in arguably the most distracting age known to humanity. It is easy to get lost in the shuffle of it all, and when we do face serious decisions, we can feel totally adrift.

Yet the God of the universe has called *you* by name. He sent his only Son to die to pay the debt of your sin so that you can experience true freedom and use that freedom well. "The glory of God is man fully alive," wrote St. Irenaeus. Your response must be to run freely with the Lord. You have been pierced by his love and want to do your part, however big or small, to bring about his kingdom here on earth. And whatever decision lies before you, you are not alone.

> *How is God speaking to your heart?*
>
> *What are the choices that lie before you?*
>
> *Do you trust in his plan?*
>
> *Will you take a step forward without knowing fully where the road will lead?*

We will face these questions and more in this book. We will look to stories of the saints and other practical wisdom for help, and we will hear the testimonies of Fr. Mike Schmitz, Jackie Francois Angel, and Bobby Angel for inspiration.

We have serious reasons to hope. God has destined us for eternity, but he has also willed that we be fully alive in him on earth! Every day we can grow closer to God so that we can listen to him and decide well, which in turn draws us ever more near to him. If a loving God is on our side, what do we have to fear?

Pray, decide, and don't worry!

HOW TO USE THIS BOOK

Sometimes we assume that discerning God's plan only matters when it comes to questions of the priesthood or religious life. You may have questions about those options, but discovering God's plan is a way of life for *all* Christians. Whatever questions you may be wrestling with, whether it is a matter of what school to attend, person to date, career to pursue, or state in life to choose, this book is meant to guide you through the process of discovering what God wants for you.

This book is a five-step "method" of finding out where God might be leading you. Just as the road to find God's will is often winding and rarely on our time schedule, this book also can be one that you do not read in a straight line.

Feel free to read through this book quickly as a "first go," but this resource will better serve you if you treat it like a road map you can pick up as needed. Slow down, wrestle with the themes, and invite God into the process of your decision making. You may need to reread certain chapters as time progresses—or put this book down altogether after a specific chapter and go live life for a while before returning to it.

We have included a journal element with some prompting questions. If you have a serious decision before you, these can help you pay attention to your thoughts and where God is leading you.

There is no substitute for a great spiritual director in your life. Seek one out if you do not have one. Pray for God to send you a priest, sister, or spiritual mentor you can trust if you have not met one yet. If your decision is a serious one, it is always beneficial to bounce it off of other people to get their perspective and also to get out of your own head.

Lastly, enjoy the journey! Life is a gift to be enjoyed, not a problem to be solved. Be patient and stay in the present moment. God will guide your steps.

Trust in the LORD with all your heart,
and do not rely on your own insight.
In all your ways acknowledge him,
and he will make straight your paths.

—PROVERBS 3:5-6

Chapter 1

SEEK

"What do you seek?"

—JOHN 1:38

THE CRY OF YOUR HEART

FR. MIKE

I remember the first time I ever saw *Superman: The Movie.* More than that—I remember exactly how it felt to walk out of the movie theater. It was this incredible experience of walking out into the summer night and wanting to do two things. I knew that I wanted to fly, and I also knew that I wanted to help people. I knew I wanted to save lives.

I remember going home that night and asking my mom and dad to tell me the truth and not sugarcoat it for me, not spare my feelings, but let me know for sure if I had been adopted. Because I thought, *Man, if I was adopted, there's a chance I could actually have come from Krypton; maybe they found me in a field somewhere, and I'm just waiting for the powers to develop.*

It turns out that I'm actually genetically a Schmitz and not adopted. Next I encountered Batman, a superhero who is completely human but trained himself and disciplined himself so he could stop criminals, save lives, and protect the innocent. I wanted to be Batman. I literally took languages in school because Batman speaks many different languages. I read detective novels so I could learn how to be a detective. I got chemistry sets because Batman was an expert chemist as well. I would physically train regularly because I wanted to be as strong and as fast as Batman.

Later I wanted to be Mitch Buchannon from the TV show *Baywatch*. I wanted to be a lifeguard, but I lived in Minnesota. I was nowhere near the ocean, where apparently these lifeguards made daring rescues every single day. All that left me with some questions: Why would God put a desire on my heart to be Superman or Batman? Why would he put the desire on my heart to be Mitch Buchannon? Why would God give me the desire to do things that weren't really possibilities for me in my life because a) I am from Earth; b) I don't have a traumatic event that is driving me to become an expert detective, an expert martial artist, an expert acrobat, an expert anything; and c) I don't live anywhere near the ocean. So why would God place something like that on my heart?

This was my first exploration of what it means to discern. After a lot of thought and reflection, I realized that just *wanting* to be Superman did not mean I was *called* to be Superman. Just because I wanted to be Batman did not mean I was called to be Batman. Just because I wanted to be a lifeguard in LA County did not mean I was called to be a lifeguard in LA County. But all of this helped me begin the process of discerning what God wanted through the desires that had been placed on my heart.

And after a lot of reflection, I recognized that all of those pieces had something in common: I've always wanted to help people. I've always wanted to be involved in saving lives. I've always wanted to be someone who is willing to sacrifice myself for the good of other people. What the Lord placed on my heart was a desire to be like him, and it wasn't until much later that I realized that the way God wanted me to live out that desire was as a priest.

———————

The very first words out of Jesus' mouth in the Gospel of John cut to the heart of the question: What are you looking for?

What is the cry of your heart? What excites you about life? What gets you out of bed in the morning? What is weighing on your mind? What are you avoiding? What are you trying to bury deep? What are you wrestling with? What are you willing to sacrifice for? How do you define a great life?

Step One in our process of discovering God's will is to seek. Whether it is a religious call, college decision, relationship issue, career change, family matter, or question of how to invest time or money, we must honestly answer Christ's question: "What am I seeking?"

It is so prevalent today to shrug off questions of deeper meaning or our purpose in the universe, but it is a lazy escape from the real issues we need to address, and we avoid them at our own peril.

We can numb ourselves with celebrity gossip, digital distractions, and creature comforts. Our material wealth in the West is unmatched, and yet suicide rates have increased by thirty percent since the 1990s. Advances in technology and the rise of social media platforms have helped our generation be more *digitally* connected, but at what cost? Many are left feeling *personally* disconnected and lonelier than ever before. Current numbers suggest that one in five college freshmen rely upon prescribed psychotropic medications to control anxiety and depression, and suicide is currently the second-most-common reason for the deaths of ten- to thirty-four-year-olds.[1]

The fact that so many prominent celebrities and Olympic athletes experience deep depression and thoughts of suicide tells us that a "complete" life does not follow from accumulating money, pleasure, or fame. "I wish people could realize all of their dreams of wealth and fame so they could see that it's not where you'll find your sense of completion," comedian and actor Jim Carrey publicly asserted.

Clearly we are meant to exist at a level deeper than what the world alone can offer us. To be fully human is to live *for something,* to have meaning, to have purpose. A person without purpose is merely existing. Too many people brimming with potential are adrift because they have not answered the central question: "What are you looking for?"

What purpose has God put on *your* heart? Do you even believe that you have a purpose? Take some honest time to reflect on your life thus far. What is stirring in your imagination and in your heart?

---

1   "Preventing Suicide," Centers for Disease Control and Prevention, 2018, cdc.gov/.

REFLECTION

- *What am I seeking?*
- *What is weighing on my mind and heart?*
- *When I am ninety years old, what will I have wanted to accomplish or regret not doing?*
- *What matters most to me?*

You have made us for Yourself,
[O Lord], and our hearts are restless
until they rest in You.

—ST. AUGUSTINE

WHO ARE YOU?

JACKIE

My senior year of high school, I thought I had it all. I was student body president, varsity volleyball captain, straight-A student, and valedictorian. I was French club president, part of the drama club board, and on the school newspaper staff. I had a great boyfriend and a full-ride academic scholarship to college. Then came the summer when my life completely changed. Maybe it was because it was a seven-day retreat instead of a three-day retreat. Maybe it was because I was surrounded by thirty other students I had never met who were all so on fire for God. Or maybe it was because we went to daily Mass, experienced Adoration, and had to memorize Scripture. Maybe, too, it was because I was challenged about my beliefs regarding some of the tough aspects of the Catholic Faith. All of that together caused a serious *metanoia*—a deep and lasting conversion of heart and mind; I encountered God like never before. I fell in love with him, and I was ready to give God everything—my vocation, my job, my tithe, my heart, my will, and my life.

That was the week I realized that who I am is not a bunch of titles or achievements. I am not my past sin. I am not my knowledge of the Faith. Who I am is a daughter of my Father. And that identity gives me great power, for the Devil fears baptized Christians who know *who* they are and *whose* they are. My heavenly Father loves me, embraces me, and wipes away every tear. My heavenly Father actually desires good for me (see Romans 8:28). So not only will he give me beautiful gifts and answer yes to my prayers, but also he will discipline me and say no to some of my desires so that I (and my desires) may be refined, purified, and made holy (see Hebrews 12:5-12).

Receiving the love of the Father has healed (and continues to heal) my wounds, my brokenness, and my hurt. No amount of achievements or titles could do that. The Father satisfies my heart and soul as water does to a land that is "dry and weary" (Psalm 63:1). No amount of followers and likes can do that. He gives me peace when the world is at war. He gives me joy and light when the culture is overcome with darkness. I cannot help but share his love, his Son, and his Spirit. I want the whole world to know what I now know—that God's love is "better than life" (Psalm 63:3).

———————

Your identity—who are you?

We are tempted to jump into this question by naming our activities, our hobbies, or our jobs.

But that is not the question.

Who are you?

Not your activities. Not your athletic ability (or lack thereof). Not your attractions or your cultural heritage. Not your achievements and not your failures. Not even your role as a parent or a spouse or a student is at the core of who you are.

Who are you?

It is a seemingly simple question but one we do anything and everything to avoid. For some of us, maybe it is just too difficult to answer. It is why we are tempted to distract ourselves with entertainment, run from silent reflection, or even numb ourselves with dangerous substances. It is the question that spins people into a midlife or quarter-life crisis. But we will never discover God's will for our lives if we never shut off the relentless noise and begin to *rest* in this profound question, which is the starting point of the journey.

We are all tempted to believe the modern lie that we are accidents in a universe of chance, "cosmic orphans," you could say. Not so. Your origin, whatever the circumstances of your family or your conception, is the result of God's love. God loves *you*. Not the nebulous "human race" but *you*, with all your quirks and oddities and scars and strengths. "Each of us is the result of a thought of God," Pope Benedict XVI asserted. "Each of us is willed, each of us is loved, each of us is necessary."[2]

Not only are we willed into this world, but we have been an eternal thought in the eternal mind of God!

Not only can I not *earn* the gift, I cannot *change* the reality of my God-given identity—neither by choice nor by the weakness of my sins. I can never lose the love of God, no matter what.

---

2   Benedict XVI, Homily (April 24, 2005), vatican.va/.

Discernment is ultimately about unearthing the will of the loving Father who has given you this profound identity. So back to the first question—who are you? For the follower of Jesus Christ, the root of your identity lies in the gift of your Baptism:

You are a beloved child of God.

The God of the universe has formed you out of nothing and called you into existence by name. You cannot earn this great gift; you can only receive it. Everything else about what you are trying to decide or accomplish must center on and return to this truth: I am willed and loved, I have a purpose, and God wants me here.

Sit with this reality. Do you believe it? Does it seem too good to be true? This truth may take time to take root in your heart. Pray for the grace to let go of the lies and receive this truth at a deep level: You are willed, you are loved, and you are necessary.

Thus says the LORD, he who created you ...
who formed you ... :
"Fear not, for I have redeemed you;
I have called you by name, you are mine."

— ISAIAH 43:1

REFLECTION

- *Who am I? (Write it out.)*
- *What gifts have I received from the Father?*
- *What activities do I usually use to define myself?*
- *What is keeping me from seeing myself as a beloved child of God?*
- *Do I struggle with seeing God as a loving Father? Why or why not?*
- ***Take It to Prayer:** I am willed, I am loved, and I am necessary. My God, help me to believe this.*

Cast all your anxieties on him,
for he cares about you.

—1 PETER 5:7

OVERCOMING FEAR

BOBBY

I remember the day I left the fire department.

I sat in my truck at the top of the fire station's parking garage, terrified of the conversation I was about to have with the chief. After working hard through the fire academy and fighting to get hired in a competitive job market, I was about to leave it all behind. *This is insane,* I thought. *God, you better be right about this.*

For years I fought God. I fought against his plan, to be more precise. Cradle Catholic by upbringing, I woke up to the truth of God's existence during my high school years and plunged headlong into his love story for my life through my college years. I came to understand my own need for healing and renewal, learning to rest in the arms of a cosmic God who knew me and loved me. I poured myself into the campus ministry programs and loved my faith and my Church for the first time.

But I still wanted to do life on my terms. I thought I knew how my life ought to pan out. I wanted to love in the way that Hollywood told me how to love. I did not want to surrender my *entire* life to God, only most of it. Yet God kept beckoning me to more. Even when I rebelled and tried to force my "ideal" life to happen, even earning a job as a firefighter, God would not leave me alone. Eventually I hit the proverbial wall. I knew that I had to follow him all the way, but I was scared.

Growing up, St. John Paul II was the only pope I ever knew. He died during my sophomore year of college. I remember crying in my dorm room, watching the news on a lousy TV. This spiritual grandfather to the world thundered again and again, "Be not afraid!" Now his words came rushing to my mind as I considered what I was about to leave behind.

With the temptation to cling to security and salary overpowering, I looked over at the center console and saw my beat-up blue Bible. I decided to play "Bible roulette" and open up to a verse at random. Maybe I would be persuaded to stay. Maybe God would give me a verse telling me I was an idiot to risk walking into the unknown, and I should just stay put.

I clearly did not know the Bible very well.

I opened to Sirach 2. This is what God smacked me with:

> My son, if you come forward to serve the Lord ... prepare yourself for temptation. Set your heart right and be steadfast ... do not be hasty in time of calamity. ... Cling to him and do not depart, that you may be wise in all your ways. Accept whatever is brought upon you ... in changes that humble you be patient. For gold and silver are tested in the fire, and acceptable men in the furnace of humiliation. Trust in God, and he will help you; hope in him, and he will make your ways straight. (Sirach 2:1-6)

I felt a sudden wave of peace overtake me. God even threw in a reference to "fire" to get me to chuckle. The fear dispersed, I left my truck with confidence and went into the fire chief's office.

"Don't tell me you're quitting" were the first words out of his mouth. I tried not to tear up as I met his eyes. It was now or never.

"I feel that God is calling me to be a priest."

As you receive this message of purpose and meaning for your life, it is important now to recognize that it will not all be smooth sailing. You will encounter storms and rocky terrain, but going headfirst into the storm and hiking difficult terrain is what is necessary in seeking God's plan and living out the call to greatness.

We are called to great things by a God who loves us, and we need to be aware that there is an enemy actively trying to derail us. One of the most effective weapons employed against us on the journey is fear, that primal force that paralyzes us in our efforts to get where we need to go.

Fear serves a purpose when we sense a threat or a dangerous situation. But fear as a survival instinct is not our focus here. We are talking about the irrational fear that bubbles up to the point where we refuse to take *any* risk and thus imprison ourselves, never becoming who we were born to be. To never risk anything is to truly never do anything. Even stepping out the front door involves a certain risk.

Fear holds us back from acting boldly. Fear convinces us to play it safe and run from risk, even risk that will likely bring about good things and a flourishing life.

New modes of fear arise if we also struggle with perfectionism or are consumed by social media. Fear of failure keeps us from attempting anything outside our comfort zone and also inflicts paralysis because we think our work will not be "perfect." Perhaps we fear success and the scary notion that we might actually succeed in our goals and have to experience the changes that will necessarily come.

Much has been written about the "fear of missing out" (FOMO), a widespread phenomenon due to the rise of social media platforms and ever-present envy of those we perceive to have more power, wealth, pleasure, or fame than we do. As we scroll through the highlights of other people's lives, we are tempted to compare ourselves, and we only perceive the places where we were not invited or are not currently traveling. We have to snap ourselves out of the endless scrolling; we have to remember to look around us and shift our focus to the good that is happening in our own lives.

We can experience a fear of commitment if we have been wounded by abuse, divorce, or betrayal and would rather attempt to guard ourselves by shutting others out and never allowing ourselves to become totally vulnerable. This can take pernicious forms, especially if we are tempted to self-sabotage what could be life-giving relationships.

So how do you overcome fear? First of all, recognize it and name it. *I experience a fear of*_____. Name whatever might be holding you back. It could be a host of fears instead of only one. That is OK. It just means that you are participating in the human condition. But you cannot let fear drive the bus forever. After naming your fear, you have to invite God in and ask for the courage to act despite your fear.

Love casts out fear. Love inspires confidence and trust; authentic love heals. Fear does not come from the Lord; it comes from the enemy of God and from our own lack of trust that God is who he says he is.

"Be not afraid!"

As you press against fear, a crucial message to remember is a phrase echoed by prophets, priests, and popes throughout the centuries: "Be not afraid!" Is it any coincidence that the simple reminder not to succumb to fear is repeated over and over again within the Scriptures? Isn't it interesting that the beloved St. John Paul II reiterated this specific message constantly in his speeches, especially when he spoke to *young people?*

Why do we need to hear these words over and over again? Perhaps because the Lord understands how powerful fear is and how easily we forget the goodness of the Lord's promises. God will deliver; we need only wait upon him and not give in to anxiety or fear.

REFLECTION

- ▶ *I experience a fear of* _____.

- ▶ *Where did this fear come from? What experiences in my life have led to this buildup of fear?*

- ▶ *What great things do I think I might be called to do?*

- ▶ *Ask God for boldness now. Ask for an increase in trust and ask that all fear may be cast out. Sit for a few minutes with this prayer. Thank the Lord for his goodness.*

Scripture to pray with:

- ▶ Psalm 118:6 – *"With the LORD on my side I do not fear. What can man do to me?"*

- ▶ Haggai 2:5 – *"My Spirit abides among you; fear not."*

- ▶ John 16:33 – *"I have said this to you, that in me you may have peace. In the world you have tribulation; but be of good cheer, I have overcome the world."*

Chapter 2

SEARCH
AND DISCERN

---

*"For every one who asks receives,
and he who seeks finds, and to him
who knocks it will be opened."*

—MATTHEW 7:8

DISCERNMENT

"Search your feelings." This well-known expression, from a popular film series set a long time ago in a galaxy far, far away, contains some mighty spiritual truth. Our emotions, reactions, decisions, and indecisions usually have an underlying current to them that we are either unaware of or afraid to face. To grow in spiritual maturity and be able to discern the road ahead requires that we slow down and sift through what is going on beneath the surface.

Take comfort in the words of Christ, who counsels us to seek and knock, for he will be with us in the searching. We will never know if we are heading in the right direction unless we search out where the Lord is moving.

We move now from Step One (seeking) to Step Two, searching and discerning our interior movements. As you think about your situation, do not be afraid to look deeper and begin to examine your inner motivations, and even your fears, to make sure that you are rightly reading the signs of the Lord in the direction you ought to walk.

FR. MIKE

Ever since I started wondering if God wanted me to be a priest, it became my preoccupation. Ever since I started actively trying to discern God's will, almost all of my praying came down to that one question: *God, what do you want me to do?* Actually it wasn't just that general question; it was very specific: *God, do you want me to be a priest, or are you calling me to marry someone?*

I would go on a retreat with the goal of answering that specific question. I would go to prayer with the goal of answering that specific question. I would pray the Rosary with the goal of answering that specific question. Every time I approached God, every time I prayed, every time I did anything that had anything to do with God, what I wanted from that event or from that prayer or from that time away was an answer to that one specific question.

Of course, God has his own timing, and he did not answer that question in any way, shape, or form for ten years. Every time I went on retreat, every time I prayed, every time I went to Mass, every time I prayed a Rosary, God was giving me graces and gifts. The problem was that I couldn't see them or I refused to see them because I wanted one thing in particular. I wanted one specific thing. I wanted an answer. I would leave every one of those retreats or prayer times upset because God did not answer my prayer.

As I look back on that, I recognize how ungrateful I was. The entire time, God was giving me himself. He was giving me graces; he was giving me the different virtues that I would need—he was giving me exactly what I needed for the moment. And I was preoccupied with what he wasn't giving me.

A massive part of discernment is recognizing that even when God doesn't give you the answer you want when you want it, he is still present. He is still working, and he calls us to return again and again to prayer, to be grateful for what he's doing and what he's giving us, and to allow him to help us according to his own time.

———————

Big Catholic word: *discernment.*

What does discernment mean, and why do people avoid doing it?

To *discern* means "to separate apart." A more amusing translation of *discern* could be "to agonize or wrestle with," which is what discernment can truly feel like. In a more positive light, it can also mean to "sift through," and that is precisely what we're doing now—sifting through all the voices to hear the voice of God better. When you discern, you sort out all the components of a particular decision: your thoughts and emotions, your head and heart, the timing and circumstances, the finances and potential hardships, the pros and cons, the opportunities and roadblocks, the risks and payoffs.

You discern when you are facing an important decision. You do not discern whether you need to turn on a light bulb, but you do discern over weighty decisions, such as your school choice, finances, career, spouse, or vocation.

To return to the central question Jesus proposed in John's Gospel, what are you looking for? What decision is weighing on you? What is preoccupying your mind and your heart? Identify that core question.

Now imagine you are dumping out onto a table all the elements of your decision. Start sorting through it all. Push your fears and worries off to the side for the moment. Look at the facts and the reality of the situation. Look at the desires welling up within you. Look at the potential regret you face if you do not follow through. Perhaps a decision will easily become clear, or you will realize that it is the wrong choice (or a right choice but the wrong time). This is the slow, agonizing work of discernment.

Before moving on, stop here and invite God, the author of your life, into your present moment. Pray this prayer often to invite the presence of God into this important process, especially in the days to come: Come, Holy Spirit.

Take a breath. Be still, and rest in God's love for you (see Psalm 46:10).

Come, Holy Spirit.

REFLECTION

▶ *What does the discernment process feel like for you right now?*

▶ *What is the "root" question that you are asking?*

▶ *If you are struggling to trust in God, why might that be?*

BETWEEN TWO GOODS

JACKIE

Have you ever met someone who looks "perfect on paper"? They are gorgeous, they have a great brain and maybe an impressive résumé and circle of friends, and even more crazy, they are super holy—but they are completely *not* the person you want to be around 24/7. Or you just do not feel like "you" when you are with them. That is pretty much how it was for me as I discerned my vocation.

When it came to the religious life, I discerned whether or not God was calling me to be a religious sister. Sure, the religious life had all the boxes checked (and, funny enough, being a sister could fit into that aforementioned list), but it did not feel like "home" to me. When I began dating, I dated some guys who had it all—the looks, the degrees, the job, the résumé, the holiness—but I absolutely did not feel peace or joy when I was with them.

Before Bobby, it always seemed as if I was trying to "make the shoe fit" with someone. It did not feel natural, nor did I feel like I could be the person God made me to be with those other guys. But when I met Bobby, I felt at home. I felt peace and joy, and I could not wait to spend time with him. I still cannot wait until he comes home every day from work. It is because I am not just in love with what Bobby is on paper—I am in love with his whole person.

The truth is, we should always be choosing between two good things. If we were discerning between a good thing and a bad thing, it would be a no-brainer. For instance, we should not date terrible people. We should be dating really amazing people whom we would recommend to our friends or who could become really great celibates (priests or religious sisters/brothers or consecrated people) and give their whole lives to God.

———————

As mentioned previously, when you discern, you face a difficult decision, and that decision usually comes down to two competing goods. If one choice was clearly the best one, it would be an easier process. When we find ourselves at the crossroads of two *goods,* we must pause and ask God for clarity in our decision making as we consider the options.

Try visualizing the two options as two doors in front of you. Consider this four-step framework of questions:

1. Is this a good door?
2. Is this an open door?
3. Is this a wise door?
4. Is this a door that you want to walk through?

If the option is not good (an unhealthy relationship, for instance), that should give you a clear answer. Is the choice even open and available? Maybe there are no jobs currently open or you received a rejection letter; that could be a clear sign. Maybe it is a good decision but not wise to move on at the present time; perhaps it will have negative consequences for those in your community if you act too quickly. Is it an option you freely desire, or do you feel forced into this decision by either the expectations of others or pressure from yourself?

These guiding questions may help you identify what is possible and life-giving for you and those around you. Perhaps you still feel "stuck" even after this exercise, though. That is OK! Discernment is a process that takes time and is rarely finished in one sitting; it can feel like a true wrestling match that will never end.

Lastly, while it may be tempting to surround ourselves with "yes-men" who will only tell us what we want to hear, we *need* real friends and family members who will tell us the truth with love (even if we do not want to hear it). Often our judgment is clouded, and we can be fickle or even rash in our decisions if we do not bounce these considerations off trusted friends. Real, virtuous friends will listen to our concerns and bring us back down to earth.

So when you stand at a crossroad, remember that God is with you and has a true desire for you to flourish, not plans to make you miserable (see Jeremiah 1:5).

My Lord God, I have no idea where I am going. I do not see the road ahead of me. I cannot know for certain where it will end. Nor do I really know myself, and the fact that I think that I am following your will does not mean that I am actually doing so. But I believe that the desire to please you does in fact please you. And I hope I have that desire in all that I am doing. I hope that I will never do anything apart from that desire. And I know that if I do this you will lead me by the right road, though I may know nothing about it. Therefore will I trust you always, though I may seem to be lost and in the shadow of death. I will not fear, for you are ever with me, and you will never leave me to face my perils alone.[1]

---

1   Thomas Merton, *Thoughts in Solitude* (New York: Farrar, Straus and Giroux, 1958), 79.

REFLECTION

▶ *What competing good choices are you facing right now?*

▶ *Imagine committing to a particular option before you, and mentally consider what the results might be. Does this bring you a sense of peace or anxiety?*

TIPS FROM ST. IGNATIUS

BOBBY

The word *fickle* made a lasting impression on me when I first learned it as a "vocab word" in high school. To be fickle is to change one's affections or loyalties frequently. I am pretty sure it was in the context of Romeo and Juliet's "love" story—a story of infatuation run amok yet hailed as true love. I could relate. For years I allowed my little romantic heart to pull me in all sorts of directions, wherever the wind blew. It all started in kindergarten with my first crush. I loved the *feeling* of love, but it sure was confusing when it came to discerning what was true. I did not learn how to "read" the movements of my heart, mind, and soul until years later.

After I entered the seminary to study for the priesthood, the rector encouraged us to learn St. Ignatius' "discernment of spirits," and so I committed myself to reading a few books on the subject. His writings made tremendous sense to me and brought much-needed guidance to my fickle heart. I remember sitting in the chapel one day and looking up from St. Ignatius' writings with a sudden burst of clarity.

Man! This sure would have helped me in college!

St. John the Evangelist wrote, "Beloved, do not believe every spirit, but test the spirits to see whether they are of God" (1 John 4:1). A spiritual director once told me, "The Lord leads; the Devil drives." When I would encounter movements of peace and stillness, I knew that God was likely blessing the place I was in, and I only needed to stay put and remain faithful. When I felt anxiety, unrest, or fear, I knew that it was a "spirit not of God," which could have been from myself, temptation, or the Devil. In those moments, I had to be still, discern what was really going on, and wait for that storm to pass. "Never make a decision in times of desolation" is one of the greatest pieces of advice St. Ignatius has given me. The ongoing journey of "testing" the movements of my mind, my heart, and my prayer grounded me in ways that I never knew before being in the seminary.

Advice like "follow your heart," while perhaps well intentioned and fitting for a two-hour romantic comedy, is subjective and likely to lead us to make some rash or even destructive decisions. It did for me. I was overjoyed when I learned there was a better way forward—I could learn to read the movements going on within my heart, discerning what was true and what was false. I and my future vocation would owe a great deal to my seminary rector and St. Ignatius of Loyola.

———

We do not need to reinvent the wheel when it comes to understanding the movements happening in our spiritual lives. A number of wise women and men have come before us and left us with treasuries of teachings. Foremost among them is St. Ignatius of Loyola.

St. Ignatius of Loyola (1491–1556) gave the Church a treasure of writings on the spiritual life upon his conversion to Christianity. He lived an ego-centered life as a military officer in his early days. After being wounded by a cannonball in battle, he lay bedridden with only the stories of the saints to read, and miraculously, he experienced a profound conversion to Christ. He devoted his life to preaching and formed his companions into the Society of Jesus (the Jesuits), which would later send missionaries across the globe.

There are "movements of the soul," as St. Ignatius called them, that we all experience. These are different from feelings or emotions; movements of the soul are deeper realities that clue us in to what God is doing deep within our souls. We experience these movements as two primary "waves" in the soul that help us identify where God is leading us: consolation and desolation.

I call it consolation when some interior movement in the soul is caused, through which the soul comes to be inflamed with love of its Creator and Lord; and when it can in consequence love no created thing on the face of the earth in itself, but in the Creator of them all.

—ST. IGNATIUS OF LOYOLA

CONSOLATION

When you are in a state of consolation, there is a palpable sensation of God's love for you. The world seems brighter, you feel a deep sense of love in your heart, and your favorite song is on the radio. Sometimes after a powerful retreat or conference, you might experience a "retreat high"—you feel that you are riding a wonderful wave of God's love and peace.

Consolation is not necessarily equated with outer happiness or comfort, though; you can be consoled by God's peace in the midst of being with the poor or downtrodden, working at a mundane job, studying for finals, or changing a stinky diaper. Consolation has to do with the deep sense of peace you receive when you are right with the Lord and are exactly where you need to be.

When you are in a state of consolation, consider the plans with which you have been wrestling. How does your heart feel when you consider the question at stake? In this grace-filled time of consolation, you can see clearly—with your head and your heart—the will of God. You are putting on the mind of Christ and can actively feel that his will and yours are in unison. This is a good state in which to consider making a decision.

There will be times of desolation—that is, times when we are not consoled—but consolation is the peace that prepares us for those inevitable valleys. It is in those times that we have to remember that consolation is reality and desolation is the illusion that I am not where the Lord wants me to be.

St. Ignatius also wrote, "Let him who is in consolation think how he will be in the desolation which will come after, taking new strength for then." The spiritual life is an ocean of waves. We cannot stay on the crest of the wave or on the mountaintop forever. Even St. Peter experienced this reality when he wanted to build tents and permanently live in that holy space of Jesus' transfiguration (see Matthew 17; Mark 9). But Jesus would not let him or his disciples rest there; on this side of heaven, we will never fully "arrive." Be thankful for moments of peace and joy, St. Ignatius affirmed, and store up these reserves of joy so that when the desert returns and consolation ends, you *remember* what the Lord has done for you.

When you are in consolation, consider the decision before you, because if you are experiencing peace and joy from God, you can see reality clearly. It is important to remember that consolation is the time that we see most clearly. We see through God's eyes, and therefore these are the times that we are encouraged to make decisions in discernment.

But as you likely guessed, there is the flip side of consolation.

I call desolation ...
darkness of soul, turmoil of spirit,
inclination to what is low and
earthly, restlessness rising from
many disturbances and temptations
which lead to want of faith,
want of hope, want of love.

—ST. IGNATIUS OF LOYOLA

DESOLATION

If there is a high, then there is also a low. The opposite of consolation is desolation, the state of being under the guidance of the "false spirit," which Ignatius attributes to anything that pulls us away from God's presence. Desolation is different from the anxiety we feel when we are in the wrong job, relationship, or place in life. Whereas the "pit in the stomach" feeling affects one aspect of our lives when all other areas are filled with joy and peace, desolation is an overarching state that can color how we view every area of our lives.

Desolation could have a few origins. Desolation can come from laziness in giving time to prayer; falling prey to lust, greed, or any other vice; or becoming mired in the hopelessness of the world. Sometimes our own psychological or emotional baggage affects us spiritually. Desolation could also come from a demonic source (remember, we Christians believe in the existence of evil, Satan, and his armies) or could be a result of temptation to evil things.

Desolation is not much fun, but God uses even this state for our good. When we are sick, our body is sending a very clear sign that something is wrong. When our soul is "sick," when something is off, God allows us to feel distant from him only to evoke the instinctual desire to return to him and his consolation.

If we are the cause of our own distance from God, consider the following questions:

- ▸ Have I committed a mortal sin or grown lazy in prayer?
- ▸ Have I stopped going to Mass or receiving the sacraments?
- ▸ What materials have I been putting into my body?
- ▸ Have I been gossiping or allowing a spirit of negativity to dominate my thoughts?
- ▸ Have I been watching pornography or movies that degrade the human person?
- ▸ Have I allowed technology to bring me to obsessing only about myself?

We can experience desolation even if we have stuck to our prayer regimen and are in a state of grace. If that is the case, it could be that God is permitting this time of darkness for our own inner purification and humility. Mother Teresa (St. Teresa of Calcutta) experienced decades of a desert-like dryness in prayer when she did not feel God's closeness. St. John of the Cross called this much more advanced stage in the life of the Christian the "dark night of the soul." It is not God's punishment—far from it—but an advanced "gift" that allows our soul to be stripped to the point where God alone can shine. For most of us, our desolation will not be so extreme, but if we follow Christ, it means that we will all share in the work of carrying his cross.

Be sure to reach out to your support network during times of desolation so you can get out of yourself and your own head. Be with friends, find good counsel, and reflect on the times when you experienced consolation. Remember that Ignatius taught us that consolation is reality, and right now we just have to stick to our plan and weather the storm.

One of the most important things regarding these spiritual movements is *never to make a decision when we are in a state of desolation.* It can be tempting to reconsider the road we are on or the progress we have made, but in this time of experiencing distance from God, we will not be thinking clearly. In desolation, we are tempted to forget about how far God has brought us and his great works. We have to imagine that we are in the middle of a storm, and the best thing to do is to lie low and wait it out.

You *will* exit desolation, but that is on God's time, not yours. Cling to Christ as your rock, make sure that you are in a state of grace, and remember that this storm will pass.

REFLECTION

- *Think back on a time when you were in a state of desolation. Describe how that felt and what you experienced.*
- *Who in your support network can you reach out to in a time of desolation?*

When one is in desolation,
he should strive to persevere in patience.
This reacts against the vexations
that have overtaken him.
—ST. IGNATIUS OF LOYOLA

One of the handiest ways to fight desolation is a fun phrase St. Ignatius would say to his followers: *agere contra.* This literally means "to act against." Some of our human tendencies are flawed, and we rightfully act against them, whether it is by exercising, not indulging in too much fast food, or learning where to cut back on obsessive technology habits.

To act against our weaknesses in the spiritual life means to put in the extra work and not take the easy road. When St. Francis of Assisi experienced his conversion and began a life of radical poverty, he was still a work in progress. The lepers in his community still repulsed him. But, moved out of conviction and love for Christ, what did he do? St. Francis kissed the wounds of a leper. He threw himself into a thorn bush when he felt sexual temptation. Over-the-top? To our modern sensibilities maybe, but St. Francis lived contrary to the ways of the world and his own fallen impulses. He allowed himself to be illuminated by God, and now we hold him up as one of our greatest saints.

If there are elements of your decision you are avoiding, you must act against your impulse and face these perhaps uncomfortable questions head-on. If you do not want to pray because you are afraid of what God might reveal to you, you must act against that fear and make time to place yourself in a position of prayer each day. You act against lust or sloth when you keep busy with constructive habits or lay aside technology so that you are present to others. Acting against your reactionary impulses will help you move forward to the right answer that you seek.

Recognize where there is inertia in your life and act against it. You may be surprised by the outcome and how the road ahead starts to become clearer. Trust in the slow work of God that is present in your life.

In the next chapter, we will move on to Step Three, the necessary and difficult step of remaining silent before the Lord.

REFLECTION

- ▶ *What uncomfortable question (or questions) are you facing right now? How can you plan to face it head-on?*
- ▶ *What are your temptations? Name them.*
- ▶ *Write out ways that you can work against* (agere contra) *your weaknesses.*

Chapter 3

SILENCE

---

*What we need most in order
to make progress is to be silent before
this great God with our appetite and
with our tongue, for the language
he best hears is silent love.*

—ST. JOHN OF THE CROSS

Does silence scare you? Many people instinctively fear silence because of the risk of repressed memories or serious questions coming to light, and we go to great lengths to avoid being left alone with our own thoughts. With the introduction of smartphones and tablets, the average adult now spends approximately three hours on mobile devices and about eleven hours a day in front of a screen.[1] In addition to keeping our memories and issues at bay, this also affects our ability to use our own creativity and imagination, navigate boredom, and, most importantly, spend time in prayer hearing the voice of God.

In Step One we set out seeking the question that God put in our hearts, and in Step Two we started searching our interior movements to discern where God might be going. As we will

---

1   Manoush Zomorodi, *Bored and Brilliant: How Spacing Out Can Unlock Your Most Productive and Creative Self* (New York: St. Martin's Press, 2017), 4.

see in this chapter, Step Three is all about embracing silence to give God an opportunity to speak.

FR. MIKE

I started discerning my vocation by asking the question "God, do you want me to be a priest?" when I was about fifteen or sixteen years old. In my mind, for a sixteen-year-old I spent a lot of time in prayer and in the church. I would seek out opportunities to pray in front of the Blessed Sacrament or go to daily Mass, but I never got a very clear answer. God never spoke to me out loud saying, "Michael, you will be a priest" or "Michael, you should get married to that girl over there. Her name is Jennifer." But once he did something very strange.

I was praying at St. Andrew's Catholic Church in Brainerd, Minnesota, minding my own business, and a woman I had never seen before came up to me and tapped me on the shoulder. She said, "I'm sorry, but I saw you in prayer. I just moved here four weeks ago, and before I moved, I had a dream, and you were in it. When I saw you praying, I realized you were the young man from my dream. In my dream, you were in the seminary. You were studying to be a priest. I just wanted to share my dream with you. … Maybe God might be calling you to be a priest or something like that."

And there I was, still kneeling, hands folded, looking up at this woman looking down at me. I smiled at her and mumbled something like, "Uh, OK, thank you," and she walked away. *OK, God, is that an answer? I don't know this woman. Maybe she's crazy, or maybe she's a visionary.*

God, what does this mean? I continued to pray, but I did not immediately know what it meant.

What do you do when something like that happens? It might be God speaking; it might not be God speaking—but you don't know what it means. This happens all the time. We pray for a sign and God gives us a sign—or does he? We pray for the intercession of St. Thérèse, and then we see a rose and think, *Oh, that's the answer—or is it?* What do you do when you don't know what something means?

Here's what you do. It's very simple—just three things: you make note of it, you consider it, and you are attentive to it.

- ▶ Note it—you might want to write it down.
- ▶ Consider it—as often as it comes up in your mind, reflect on it and ask yourself if this resonates with what you know.
- ▶ Be attentive to it—in a sense, you do your best not to forget it.

That moment, that woman telling me about her dream, was not the answer. But it was enough for me to keep asking, "God, is this what you want?"

Here's a little epilogue to this story. Years later after I had actually gotten ordained, a young man came up to me and said, "Hey, my aunt says she's responsible for you becoming a priest." I was like, "What, seriously?" He said, "Yeah, my aunt said she told you once that she had a dream where you were a priest and that's why you're a priest now." I had completely forgotten the story, and it had not played any role whatsoever in my decision to enter the seminary. When she shared her message with me, it motivated me to keep praying, but it in no way made me go into the seminary when the time actually came to join. But it did serve a purpose: it taught me that when I don't know what something means, I will note it, consider it, and be attentive to it.

Each of us has some kind of vocation. We are called by God to share in his life and in his Kingdom. Each one of us is called to a special place in the Kingdom. ... For each one of us, there is only one thing necessary: to fulfill our own destiny, according to God's will, to be what God wants us to be.[2]

—THOMAS MERTON

UNDERSTANDING VOCATION

Let us look at another important Catholic word: *vocation*. From the Latin *vocare* we get "call" or "summon" (think of our modern words *vocal* or *voice*). A vocation is not something we rightfully choose for ourselves but some action or way of life that draws us in and gives us life. Think of an athlete who excels at a sport or an artist losing herself in her craft. Sure, there are still hours of practice required, and the effort is not always enjoyable, but the activity—or the state of life to which we are called—truly brings us life and gives life to others.

2 Thomas Merton, *No Man Is an Island* (New York: Houghton Mifflin Harcourt, 1983), 131.

For a Christian, there is an even deeper understanding of vocation. A central theme that occurs again and again in the Bible is "called by name." Remember your identity from Chapter 1? God has called you by *name*, not as a random speck in the universe but as an unrepeatable individual with something special to contribute to the earthly world and to the kingdom of God. The fundamental call of *every* person is to love. God, who is love, has created us out of love and for love.

Even more than an action, your vocation is who you are called to *be!* Hearing the call is simply uncovering who you already are and remembering that identity. From this identity will flow your eventual mission or particular task.

However, one of the crucial points of being able to hear a call is having the ability to *listen.*

God is usually subtle. He does not barge into our lives with lightning bolts like Zeus or with the hammer of Thor. Our Lord is a gentleman who leads with "a still small voice" (1 Kings 19:12). Mother Teresa would often say that God speaks the loudest in silence. But if we do not make room for silence, we will never hear the call of the Good Shepherd (see John 10:11).

Most of us are far from farms and do not work with livestock, but it is amazing to hear about the variety of calls and whistles shepherds use to get the attention of their flocks. Sheep, who have a reputation of not being very smart, can differentiate between the calls of neighboring shepherds and learn to discern their own shepherd's distinct call.

We must eliminate all other competing voices in order to hear the voice of *our* shepherd, Jesus Christ. Now more than ever, we must make an effort to switch off the distractions and noise so we can better know ourselves, discern the movements of our souls, and recognize the voice of God.

How will you know it is the voice of God and not your own mind? That takes trial and error, but God created your mind, and he can and does speak to you through your imagination. Sometimes you will receive such clarity in a particular thought or word that you sense it is God speaking. Another time you might suddenly have a seemingly "random" memory or thought about a friend who needs prayer. The closer you are to the Scriptures and the more you carve out daily space for prayer, the more clearly you will hear his voice.

Switch off the noise today. Have the courage to be still.

REFLECTION

- ▶ *Where or when do you struggle to embrace silence?*

- ▶ *What thoughts and memories are stirred up when you are silent?*

- ▶ *Challenge yourself to sit in silence for at least ten minutes (or longer). Set a timer so you do not cheat. Do not read or engage in some other activity. When your mind wanders, simply return to the thought of God, and ask him in trust for the grace to be brought back into his presence. Know that he is eager to speak to you.*

"For I know the plans I have for you, says the LORD, plans for welfare and not for evil, to give you a future and a hope."

—JEREMIAH 29:11

YOUR PRESENT MOMENT IS NOT A WASTE

JACKIE

We all know the phrase "The grass is always greener on the other side." Well, it should really say, "We *think* the grass is always greener on the other side. But really the grass is greener where you water it."

I often tell single people who are feeling dissatisfied with their state in life that miserable single people make miserable married people. If you want a healthy and holy marriage, you need to be a healthy and holy person. So if you are miserable and unhealthy and unholy now, you absolutely will be miserable later when you think that some earthly thing or some other person will change you or fix you.

I say this because people (including myself) often try to deal with today's hurts with tomorrow's promises. We say things like "I'll be happy *when* so-and-so happens" or "I'll be happy *if* so-and-so happens." How about just being happy *today* because tomorrow is not promised? And how about recognizing that no earthly thing can satisfy an unearthly ache?

Since my conversion at eighteen, I have tried to live this out. I was a very joyful single person who was in love with

God. I knew that God alone satisfied my heart and soul, and no other person or thing could satisfy every desire of my heart. So every day while my heart ached and longed to be in my vocation, I reminded myself to let that ache be transformed into prayer to God. I prayed Psalm 63 often, and I rejoiced that God was with me, next to me, in me. I had to remember that my life did not start once I got married. My life was happening now, and God was calling me to be a "gift of self" to every person I met.

God was calling me to love and to serve. God was calling me to be holy, so I went to daily Mass. I went to confession often. I sat with Christ in Adoration. I read, studied, and digested the Word of God. And I waited for God's call.

I did not know if my call to marriage would come at age twenty-eight or at fifty. But I knew I would rather be single and joyful in God than be miserable in a marriage I called myself to. So I waited day by day, doing the will of God and allowing him to satisfy me, heal me, comfort me. And I want every person to know it is possible to be "in the waiting" while also being fully joyful and alive in the present, because each of us has the One who is the greatest gift of all.

————

Your time right now is not a waste.

Right now, in this very moment, your life is happening.

It is tempting to feel as if you are in a state of limbo or some kind of "holding pattern" as you discern the next step to take. For instance, maybe all the Lord wants you to do right now is be a college student and nothing more yet. Instead of fixating on a future that has not happened yet or beating yourself up over your past mistakes, focus on the present moment. That is where God is—and that is where he wants you to stay.

Your life does not begin once you are married or take vows or buy a house or retire or … on and on. You are living your life *now*! You have time right now to develop your skill sets, read, write, travel, pray, serve. Every season of life brings with it new deaths and new life, new challenges and new opportunities.

The present moment is a valuable time of training for whatever the Lord has in store ahead.

Look at yourself today and be honest with where you are and where you need to grow. Where are you lazy or slothful? Where do you indulge in lust? Where does your greed or envy manifest itself? Do you spend too much time on your phone or on social media? Where does your pride rear its ugly head? Is your prayer life what it ought to be? Is serving the Lord priority one in your life? Where can you be more generous? Really take a hard look at yourself. Seriously, write your answers down—*now*.

Begin working on these areas of your life *today*, not tomorrow. The best gift you can give to your future vocation is to sanctify your present day. We grow in holiness and virtue in the quiet, unnoticed, and underappreciated moments of each day.

You may feel as though you are waiting for your "real life" to begin, but remember, your life has already begun; it is unfolding day by day. So get living and leave the rest up to God.

You are on the way. You are already on the journey. Stay focused on your current step, and make sure it is the best footing for the next.

For today, be right where you are.

REFLECTION

► *Do you struggle to stay in the present moment?*

► *If so, what is pulling at your attention?*

► *How can you be more present in the moment?*

*The present moment holds infinite riches
beyond your wildest dreams. ... The
will of God is manifest in each moment,
an immense ocean which the heart only
fathoms in so far as it overflows with
faith, trust, and love.*[3]

—JEAN-PIERRE DE CAUSSADE

LONELINESS

BOBBY

Praying in the seminary chapel one evening, my mind returned to a moment of profound loneliness I had experienced during my college years. I remembered heading back to my dorm late one night, walking up the hill near our basketball stadium and staring up at the night sky. Tired of falling into the same sinful habits over and over again and tired of waiting for God's plan to be revealed for my life, I prayed an ardent prayer of longing, an existential cry to be seen and known by this God who supposedly loved me and yet was so silent.

I felt that restless ache of my heart in an overwhelming way like never before.

My friend David, who is now a priest, would tell me years later that loneliness is just God knocking on the door of your heart asking you to spend time with him. While I wanted to write that off as a cheesy sentiment, his words pierced my heart. How many times had I turned

---

3 Jean-Pierre de Caussade, *The Sacrament of the Present Moment* (New York: Harper & Row Publishers, 1989), 62.

to passing pleasures and distractions in moments of loneliness rather than still myself and rest in the presence of God? Even when I felt direction from the Lord, that ache never went away.

Returning to my time in the seminary, we had a guest lecturer who presented on St. John Paul II's "Theology of the Body," a profound work detailing how our bodily creation as human persons echoes God's love for us and call to communion. During a question-and-answer session, I asked the speaker how—as a seminarian—I could channel the longings I felt for fatherhood and how these desires could be fruitful. I will never forget his answer—mostly because I did not like it:

"You have to stay in that ache. You have to bring those desires to the Lord and rest in that longing."

What the *heck* did that mean?

I longed to be a spouse, and I longed to be a father. But I had to realize that this was all in God's time, not my own. I had to enter into that "stretching" of my heart and allow Christ to transform my life and my loneliness. It was tough. Some days were frustrating, and many days prayer was dry. But I grew in that stretch, and I am a better man because of it.

Pope Benedict XVI, when he was Cardinal Joseph Ratzinger, wrote that "the Fathers of the Church say that prayer, properly understood, is nothing other than becoming a longing for God."[4] St. Teresa of Avila also

---

4   Hans Urs von Balthasar and Joseph Cardinal Ratzinger, *Mary: The Church at the Source*, trans. Adrian Walker (San Francisco: Ignatius Press, 2005), chapter 1, Google Books.

wrote that God hears us not with the noise of words but with our longing. Sometimes God allows our hearts to be broken so that he might mend and fill them.

I learned to embrace solitude and, I daresay, love the stretch. Even today I still experience that ache within my heart. But that ache means that I am alive and not satisfied by this world alone. God is knocking, and I must respond.

––––––––––

In taking time for silence and sitting with the present moment, we may encounter feelings of loneliness. This is OK! Loneliness comes to us all. Do not think you are abnormal if you find yourself with a feeling of loneliness. It is part of the human experience.

Sometimes we feel lonely after a great loss or when we are in a new environment, perhaps that first feeling of being "homesick." At other times we may have no reasonable explanation for feeling lonely; we might be in a crowded room of people or at a party and feel profoundly alone.

We all tend to run from this feeling of being lonely and want to escape it by any means necessary. We can all fall prey to "counterfeit loves" that dull the experience of this "ache": base entertainment, mindless Internet scrolling, overspending, gossip, pornography, alcohol or substance abuse, and so on.

St. John Paul II described loneliness as "original solitude," the deep sense that we as humans stand alone in the universe as wholly different from the animals, plants, and stars. We share something with creation, and yet we have a very different place in creation. We can sense being "set apart," and this naturally creates a sense of loneliness.

Remember the "cry of the heart" from our first chapter? This is the cry of creation: Who am I?

In a real way, the ache of loneliness is a great gift, because it pierces the heart with the conviction that we were made for *communion*—literally, "union with another." We were not made to be alone—we were made in the image and likeness of a God who is a communion of Persons: Father, Son, and Holy Spirit. Only in relationship with others do we "make sense." Our desire, especially sexual desire, is often the ache for eternity written into our souls.

Remember, loneliness is just God knocking on your heart asking you to spend time with him. When you experience loneliness, it is really a cry for God to remember your identity.

Solitude and rest are vital for recollection; they are vital for the human soul. It is a sign of unhealthiness if you can never be by yourself in a quiet room. What is more, you are never fully alone—the God of the universe, the God of the present moment, is closer to you than you realize—closer than your very breath. When loneliness strikes you in your decision-making process, remember that God knows you, loves you, and is present to you.

What you do with loneliness is important. Recognize it, feel it, and redirect your energies. Do not run from the ache. Face your loneliness and enter into it, asking the Lord to be with you. Visualize Christ being with you in the darkness. Trust him to reveal his heart and will to you. Then listen.

Do not be afraid if all you seem to hear is silence. Sometimes the "silence" of God that we experience in prayer is a simple affirmation that we are where we need to be. God wants us to simply "be" and not overthink the work he has right in front of us. God's silence in prayer can be a simple message of "you are where I need you to be, and when I want you to move, you will know it."

In the next chapter, you'll move on to Step Four, sorting out all the data you've collected to date. But don't rush on just yet. Sit in the silence. Have the courage to sit with God in times of loneliness and refuse to run to any other substitute.

God is with you in this process.

REFLECTION

▶ *Recall a time when you felt lonely. Describe that time and what you did about it.*

▶ *Pray with this question: "Is God enough for me?" If everything in your life were to be taken away, would the love of God be enough for you?*

ST. IGNATIUS' *SUSCIPE* PRAYER

*Take, Lord, and receive
all my liberty, my memory, my
understanding, and my entire will,
all I have and call my own.
You have given all to me.
To you, Lord, I return it.
Everything is yours;
do with it what you will.
Give me only
your love and your grace,
that is enough for me.*

Chapter 4

SORT

Discernment itself should not
be a stiff, brittle, anxious thing, but—
since it too is part of God's will for our
lives—loving and joyful and peace-filled,
more like a game than a war,
more like writing love letters
than taking final exams.

—PETER KREEFT

At this stage in the game, you have looked inward at your central question. You have sat with some central truths of your identity as a beloved son or daughter of God, and you know the Lord is with you in this process. You have examined your thoughts, emotions, and fears. You have spent time in silence to assess what is going on beneath the surface, and you have given God the chance to speak.

We arrive now at Step Four in this discernment process: Sort out the data. Imagine a table set before you with all of the information you've collected spread across it. Now you must sort through it all and sift out where you think God is directing your steps.

FR. MIKE

Back in the day, NBC sports would regularly have an episode once a year devoted to the Ironman World Championship Triathlon in Kona, Hawaii. I remember seeing this every year as a kid. It was one of the things that my parents and my siblings and I were excited to watch together. We weren't really a sit-down-and-watch-sports kind of family, but we all ran, we all swam competitively, we all rode bikes, and we were all cross-country skiers. So watching the Ironman Triathlon was right up our alley.

The first time I ever watched an Ironman, I remember thinking, *I want to do that race someday.* The winners' stories were cool, but it was the stories of the average, everyday racers that captivated me the most. They were normal human beings doing something extraordinary. It made me want to do something extraordinary as well. My dad had always run marathons. My mom also did marathons—running as well as cross-country skiing marathons. My dad at that point had already done a half Ironman Triathlon, and my siblings and I had participated in short-course triathlons. But the idea of actually completing the entire Ironman Triathlon—2.4 miles of swimming, 112 miles of biking, and 26.2 miles of running—was exciting. The idea was so inspiring, I knew that at some point I wanted to participate in that race as well.

There is a difference, of course, between wanting to do something and actually choosing to do it. There's a difference between having a dream and having a goal. There's a difference between getting excited by something and actually taking the steps to accomplish it. Taking action is absolutely necessary. I can have a dream. I can have a vision. I can have a hope, but until I take those steps, until I move on that dream or take action on that hope, it all remains just a dream. This is true whether it's the idea of running a race or having a relationship with God or helping people or marrying someone or entering the seminary or convent.

It wasn't until I said, "OK, when's the first race I can participate in?" and then said, "OK, what do I need to do in order to be ready for that race?" that my dream began to become a reality. Taking smaller steps helped clarify for me whether this was actually something I wanted. It's easier to participate in a triathlon with a 500-meter swim versus 2.4 miles in the Ironman, a 15-mile bike versus 112 miles, and a 5-mile run versus 26.2 miles. Taking those initial steps is saying, "OK, this is a dream, but is it really a goal? This is something I would like to do, but is it something I actually *will* do?"

Taking action clarifies; taking action purifies. Taking action becomes a test of whether you really want something or it's just a nice idea. It's not a matter of whether you are tough enough to do something; it's a matter of clarifying your intention and purifying your desire. If I were to sign up to do the Ironman because I thought that I would get a lot of attention for it or because I'd win, that would be the wrong reason because I am not that fast. I'm not that good. I'm definitely a middle-of-the-pack triathlete. But taking action purifies that desire, and the same thing is true for any vocation. Until we take action on pursuing a vocation, our intention is still muddy, and our desires are still mixed. But when we begin to take action, very quickly our intentions become clearer and our desire—what we are truly looking for—becomes more and more purified.

SMALL STEPS

For the moment, let go of the all-or-nothing approach. Take some incremental steps.

Sometimes you are able to make a low-risk choice instead of betting it all at once. This can often be the wiser option when you are wrestling with a big decision. You may not need to quit your job in order to examine the next opportunity. Perhaps you can start dabbling in that new field of work, visit that school, or simply date that person you are interested in to see if you *actually* enjoy it. Part of this process is to "come and see"; you are not taking a blood oath of fidelity to this option.

A small step will often give you clarity as to whether or not this is an option worth going "all in" on.

But God cannot work if you never move. Sometimes we have "vocational paralysis" (the business world calls it "analysis paralysis"). We are too afraid of making a mistake, and so we never make a move in any direction, desperately seeking some kind of absolute certainty. This choice to not make a decision is, ironically, a decision. Sadly, we are cutting off every option because we are too scared to pursue any option.

In most cases you will never have *absolute* certainty. You can never be sure of anything to come in the next day, good or ill. Christ tells us to step out in faith and be not afraid: "Therefore do not be anxious about tomorrow, for tomorrow will be anxious for itself. Let the day's own trouble be sufficient for the day" (Matthew 6:34).

Consider this question as well: What is the cost of *not* doing this?

Will you regret shutting the door on the opportunity before you?

There will always be curveballs thrown your way that you cannot plan for. Will you be faithful and take a small step to move forward with the information that God has given you?

Discernment is a fluid process, one not always set in stone. We may choose a decision wisely, but there are always moments when perhaps we must change course and (unfortunately) begin the process again. The process of discernment is a way of life, not a once-in-a-lifetime process. Discernment is linear, but it is also cyclical. Yet we'll never get into motion if we never take action.

Do not "discern your decision to death" with inaction. Take a breath. You do not have to have everything figured out right now.

Make one small decision today.

REFLECTION

- *Is there an opportunity in front of you that you might regret not pursuing?*

- *What small step can you take today, trusting God for the next one tomorrow?*

Nothing is more practical
than finding God,
than falling in love
in a quite absolute, final way.
What you are in love with,
what seizes your imagination,
will affect everything.
It will decide what will get you
out of bed in the morning,
what you do with your evenings,
how you spend your weekends,
what you read, whom you know,
what breaks your heart,
and what amazes you
with joy and gratitude.
Fall in love, stay in love,
and it will decide everything.

ATTRIBUTED TO
FR. PEDRO ARRUPE, SJ
(1907–1991)

YOU CAN'T DO IT ALL

JACKIE

My first job out of college was a youth ministry position a mile from a Southern California beach. I lived in a two-bedroom condo owned by the church I worked for, so my rent was super cheap. I even had a decent income, but really, after college, anything above five dollars in my checking account made me feel like a rich woman! And I did not go hungry, either. (In fact, I probably gained ten pounds from eating pizza all the time.) I loved the parishioners, the people I worked with, and the job itself.

A few months into the job, a Catholic recording label asked me to be one of their new artists. They wanted me to come out with an album of my original music. I thought, "All of these Catholic musicians and songwriters are either full-time traveling 'itinerant' ministers or music ministers. None of them are youth ministers. How do I do this?" At first I thought that I could totally do this music thing and still be a youth minister. I had already traveled out of state a few times while in college to lead music for retreats or speak to teens. So I could still do this while being a youth minister, right?

But something kept nagging me. I started feeling anxiety in my job. I started experiencing a lot of restlessness. About ten months into my youth ministry job, I would wake up and feel sick to my stomach even thinking about work. I don't know about you, but when God wants me to move into a job or out of a relationship, I get an anxious feeling in the pit of my stomach. When I finally listen to God and move, that anxiety goes away. In this instance, my head was saying, "Are you kidding? You want to give up a steady paycheck and beach living to move back in with your parents and become a full-time traveling musician/preacher when you do not even know when or if you will ever get asked to do events?" My heart, on the other hand, was saying, "Move. Go. Listen to that anxiety. Take that leap of faith. God has something better for you." Sure enough, I took that leap of faith. I prayed, "God, if this is what you are calling me to do, I know you will provide!"

And you know what? He did. He always does. But we have to be willing to take the leap.

––––––––––

Many of us think that we are great at multitasking, but in reality, we are not doing any one thing very well at all.

We can have seventeen tabs open in our Internet browser yet not be attentive to any of them. We think we can master the skill of looking at a phone, drinking coffee, studying for a class, and "listening" to the friend sitting next to us—all at the same time—but we fail miserably at being attentive to any one thing.

We have been told that we can "do it all," and so we try. And we fail. Horribly.

While you might be able to do almost anything, you cannot do *everything*.

You cannot do it all; you simply cannot. But that is OK. Because in committing to one or two things, you can and will find a great freedom.

By trying to keep all our options open and never committing to *one* thing, we actually miss out on *all* things. We do many things poorly instead of throwing ourselves into one thing well. We may even refrain from committing to events with friends, always waiting instead for something better to come along. This strategy (which is often unconscious) initially may seem to lead to a more carefree life, but it leads to an extremely distracted, flaky, and insecure existence in the long run.

The Latin word *decidere* (where we get the modern word *decide*) means "to cut off." Whenever we decide on something, we are cutting off the other possible options. If we are meant to live life deeply, then we must start by examining what is on the table and eliminating what is unnecessary. Not everything is good. In fact, sometimes the good is the enemy of the great.

Before you start hyperventilating, consider an example. When a man says yes to loving his wife and committing himself to her alone, he also says no to loving any other woman in such a romantic way. Committing that "yes" to his wife in a total way is indeed an exercise of freedom that produces great happiness and peace as opposed to living life forever on the fence. As St. John Paul II would affirm, man can only find himself through a sincere gift of self.

If you experience a fear of commitment and if the thought of making definitive choices scares you, you're not alone. But we must realize that to totally commit to an endeavor is a great good—one that *frees* our energies to be devoted with singular energy to one goal. Commitment means exercising our freedom in a profound way, not reducing it.

Execute. Do *something*. Life will not necessarily go according to your twenty-, ten-, or five-year plan. You need to start living. Your first job is just that—a job—and it will not be the career that fulfills you for all eternity (no job ever will). Your college years may start out well, but you may need a change later. The first date is a first date, not a blood oath for marriage. Decisions can change. But we must first decide.

Do one thing. Do that well.

REFLECTION

- *What are the options on my plate right now?*
- *Are there unnecessary things in my life that I could drop?*
- *What decision am I struggling with?*
- *If I am experiencing a fear of commitment, what might be behind it?*

The Lord has a plan for each of us,
he calls each one of us by name.
Our task is to learn how to listen,
to perceive his call, to be courageous
and faithful in following him and,
when all is said and done, to be
found trustworthy servants who have
used well the gifts given to us.[1]

—POPE BENEDICT XVI

CAN I MAKE THE WRONG CHOICE?

BOBBY

It has been said that ever since *discerning* became a fashionable word, no one has decided anything. My story certainly echoes this.

My twenties were dominated by the "what does God want from me?" question, but I was often so stuck in my head and so terrified to make the wrong decision that I would not make any decision. I tried to date, but I was bogged down by the fear that I could not totally give myself over to anyone until the priesthood question was answered, and I hurt several friends in the process. I made the mistake time and time again of treating God like a Magic 8 Ball that would tell me my path if I waited long enough.

But that is not how God operates. God respects our freedom way too much.

---

1   Benedict XVI, Homily (September 11, 2006), vatican.va/.

In the years that would follow my seminary journey, God gave me an amazing spiritual director who helped me discern that my call was indeed to marriage, to be a husband and a biological father. Shortly afterward I reconnected with Jackie and, after what seemed like eons of endless waiting on God's will, everything fell into place quickly. I pursued her and proposed, and thank the Lord she said yes. An awesome job and the blessing of children followed shortly thereafter.

Since becoming a parent, I have had many "aha" moments when it comes to learning more about the fatherhood of God. I delight when my children achieve things on their own. I delight when they create and explore and dance and get dirty and make mistakes. I delight when they can stand on their own and when they are so tired that I get to carry them to bed. I delight when *they choose* their course of action and learn along the way. I believe that God operates in the same way.

God has been with me in whatever I have decided throughout my life, even when I decided poorly. He was always waiting to write straight with my sideways lines. But he also delighted in the fact that I was acting and *in motion*. A friend pointed out to me that we honor God when we choose without total clarity, because we are effectively saying, "Listen, God, I cannot see the whole path, but *I trust you*, and I know you will redirect me as needed." When my children jump off the stairs into my arms, it is a bizarre way of honoring me, because they are saying, "I trust you'll catch me, Dad!" They honor me along with giving me a heart attack!

Will you choose poorly? Probably, but so did I. That is how we learn.

God wants you to choose. And we honor him when we do so.

———————

What if I decide poorly?

What if I work against the plan God has for me?

What if I screw up my life beyond all repair?

If any of these questions have popped up in your mind, relax—you are normal. But allowing these questions to drive your whole process will keep you trapped in fear and a paralyzed state.

They are good questions, though.

God does not want us to be robots; he wants human persons who freely choose to love. Thus, we have the ability to be acting agents in our story. As parents delight when their children learn to walk, draw, and ride a bike, God delights in us as we use our gifts, talents, and abilities to love and serve others. God never manhandles us into a decision, but he will work within our desires and circumstances to exert some pressure at times to guide us where we will most flourish.

We can choose not to cooperate with his plan, of course. Our own self-centeredness and sin can cause us to ignore or totally miss the signposts God presents, and we can choose to chart our own course, even if it leads to self-destructive tendencies and serious consequences.

God will never write you off, however. God is the relentless lover of his prodigal sons and daughters, and he constantly writes straight with our crooked lines.

Consider the modern-day metaphor of a GPS device. I might see the path ahead, but I can deviate and take my own route. The GPS recalibrates, constantly trying to get me back on course. I have the freedom to cooperate with the GPS or not. Likewise, God constantly recalibrates in alignment with our choices, respecting our freedom while guiding us at various intervals toward his ideal path for us. For our part, we must be open to his guidance, becoming aware of it through prayerful listening to his voice.

Reject any spirit of fear or the voice of the Evil One, who might suggest that God will not be with you in the outcome you choose. Assuming that you are taking this process to prayer, collaborating with others, and striving for holiness, you will not choose wrongly. Perfect love casts out all fear, and you have a God who is desperately in love with you.

REFLECTION

▶ *Think of a time when you were not sure you were making the right decision. How was God present with you? How did he guide you?*

▶ *How is God calling you to exercise the power of choice today?*

There is no fear in love, but perfect love casts out fear. For fear has to do with punishment, and he who fears is not perfected in love. We love, because he first loved us.

—1 JOHN 4:18-19

Chapter 5

STEP OUT

___

*God has created me
to do some special service;
God has committed some work
to me which has not been
committed to another.
I have a mission.*

—JOHN HENRY CARDINAL NEWMAN

We have worked through Steps One through Four, and now only Step Five remains: to step out into the unknown. As you stand at a crossroads, this is the inevitable point you are either anticipating or dreading—the moment of action.

While it might be safer to keep all these points of discernment within the comfortable walls of your own mind, life is not safe, and we're not meant for comfort. We are meant for greatness.

FR. MIKE

I asked God almost every day for ten years whether or not he wanted me to be a priest. I remember telling him very clearly, "God, I don't care what it is; just let me know what you want me to do. I don't care if you want me to get married. I don't care if you want me to be a priest. I just want to know."

But God did not tell me. I didn't have any degree of certainty after praying for ten years. And then, at a certain point God simply made it very clear in a subtle and organic way that the next step for me was to enter the seminary. I didn't know about anything after that. I didn't know if he wanted me to go all the way through it. I didn't know if he wanted me to go to seminary just to try it out. All I knew was that he wanted me to go to seminary. The most amazing thing about that was not finally knowing. The most amazing thing for me was that my heart was ready the moment he told me. I remember thinking, *Wow, if God had told me this even three weeks earlier, I think it would have felt like trying to fit a round peg in a square hole.* I would have pounded away at it to make it fit, but it wouldn't have been joyful. It wouldn't have had the same kind of love and excitement and zeal, and God knew this.

I kept telling him, *I'm ready, I'm ready, I'm ready.* But God, being God, is very wise and omniscient, and he knew the right timing. You might think, *I'm ready. Just tell me, God—I can face the music.* But God loves you and wants your good. God loves you too much to let you know ahead of time what you're not ready for. God will not reveal his call for you a moment too late, but he won't reveal it a moment too early.

———————

TRUSTING IN GOD

In a message for the youth of the Church—in particular, seminarians—Pope Benedict XVI affirmed the need to commit oneself wholeheartedly to the journey ahead:

> *A true education must awaken the courage to make definitive decisions, which today are considered a mortifying bind to our freedom. In reality, they are indispensable for growth and in order to achieve something great in life, in particular, to cause love to mature in all its beauty: therefore, to give consistency and meaning to freedom itself.* [1]

Plowing ahead and pursuing anything of importance in life absolutely requires some measure of risk. Whether it is asking a person on a date, picking a major to study, or deciding to pursue a religious calling, there will always be a risk. You cannot live life totally averse to risk; that is certainly no way for a follower of Christ to live.

Many of those in our grandparents' and great-grandparents' era risked life and livelihood to fight in global wars or emigrate to foreign lands with little more than the clothes on their backs. Our ancestors had no idea what the outcome would be or what tomorrow would bring, but they acted anyway despite the associated risks. Let us not be known as the "paralyzed generation," the era too afraid ever to make a decision.

Remember that after great risk often comes great reward.

---

1   Benedict XVI, Address to the Participants in the Fourth National Ecclesial Convention (October 19, 2006), vatican.va/.

For us Christians, what have we to fear? Christ has poured out upon us his Holy Spirit so that we might grow in boldness, wisdom, and all the spiritual gifts. Our God has beaten even death itself! What have we to fear?

On the topic of death, consider the Latin phrase *memento mori,* which translates to "remember your death." This is not a call to have an unhealthy, morbid fixation but rather a wake-up call to rebuke the lie that we can be forever young or can get away with avoiding important decisions. We will all die; what will we do with our days between now and then? How will we live in the here and now?

Do not fear the possibility of failing more than the possibility of winning something amazing. We are not meant to live life in a perpetual holding pattern. Failure is not the opposite of success; failure is part of success. Failure motivates us to refine our path. It builds character and dependence on God and helps us unlock our true potential.

Eventually you have to trust God and your own evaluation of your situation and step out of the abstract into the great unknown.

REFLECTION

- ▶ *What risks are you afraid to take?*
- ▶ *Whom do you look up to or admire for their courage?*

YOUR VOCATION IS NOT ABOUT YOU

JACKIE

Growing up, I did not want to be a mom. I had a lot of friends who cooed over babies and desired motherhood more than anything. I, on the other hand, wanted to be a princess. I desired to have a personal cook, masseuse, maid, hairstylist, makeup artist, and clothing stylist. I did not want to take care of others; I wanted others to take care of me. I always thought kids were annoying and needy. And I probably thought that because (1) they are, and (2) having kids would compete with my annoying neediness. It was not until I met Bobby that I desired to have kids, because I wanted *Bobby's* kids. I wanted kids like him. And yes, while our kids are annoying and needy in this toddler stage, they are *my* annoying and needy kids, and I love them. Every day these little mutants teach me to be selfless. They are drawing me out of my selfishness and teaching me how to sacrifice and how to love. I am still a total brat some days and get frustrated and frazzled by how exhausting it is to be a mother and always on demand when I just want to chill and read a book and drink my coffee, but I also know that I will rest in heaven … and maybe when my kids are adults. Maybe.

Even though I discerned being a religious sister, I can look back and see that God was calling me to be married and to be a mom because that is how he would be able to purify my selfish heart the best. That is how he would be able to draw love out of me. And while it is exhausting and seemingly unending, I know that life is short, and this is a tough stage of motherhood I am in right now.

But in the midst of cleaning poopy diapers and dealing with tantrums that sound like demonic possession, I am forming little saints. I am teaching them to love God and love their neighbor as themselves, and they are teaching me the same.

And it is worth every second.

———————

At this point, it is good to remember that your life is ultimately not about you. It is easy to approach big decisions as if the world centers around you and all that matters is your personal fulfillment, self-actualization, or mere happiness. But God does not call you to a life of isolation or self-centered egoism. Remember your identity, from our discussion in the very first chapter. God is calling you to himself.

After graduating from college in 1990, Christopher McCandless left all his personal belongings and wealth, traveled across North America, and hitchhiked to Alaska in April 1992. Inspired by the likes of Henry David Thoreau and Ralph Waldo Emerson, he set out with minimal supplies to reject society as he knew it and live in isolation off the land, out of contact and away from aid from any other people. One of his last journal entries, before he died of still-unknown causes, contains the pertinent revelation that cuts to the core of how we are created in the image of a communal God: "Happiness Real When Shared."[2]

During a podcast interview, actor Will Smith affirmed this deep truth that we are made for others:

2 Jon Krakauer, *Into the Wild* (New York: Anchor Books, 1997), 189.

I've been to the top of money. ... I've had all of the adoration. I've been to the top of all those material world mountains, and nothing makes you happy other than being useful to others. That's it. That's the only thing that ever will satisfy that thing, is that what you're doing is useful.[3]

Have I lived my life in a way that serves others? How have I been made to love our Lord the best? How will the decision that I am about to make glorify him? This is what my life and ultimately my discernment have always been about.

We prove our love to Jesus by loving as he did: selflessly. Without expectation of reward, we must give. It is the great paradox of life that only in losing our lives will we truly find ourselves and discover who we are meant to be. St. Thérèse of Lisieux, the "Little Flower," asserted that above all else, her vocation was simply to love. How will the big decision ahead of you enable you to love?

Now that you have discerned and arrived at the point of action, it does not mean that life will be all butterflies and soft pillows from here on out. Periods of challenge and discomfort will still arise. You may find yourself in times of trial or with people who rub you the wrong way. That is good! It is OK to be uncomfortable. These are opportunities of growth, necessary for both your personal maturation and, more importantly, your holiness. During such times of discomfort, stop and ask God, "What are you trying to teach me here?" The answer may surprise you.

---

3   Will Smith, Episode 39, July 4, 2018, in *Rap Radar*, produced by Tidal, podcast, rapradar.com/.

Making a decision will not solve every ache in your heart or every desire that longs to be satisfied. And you will always have a deep ache—a desire for God, a longing for his love—that only he can fill.

Where God calls you, when approached rightly, will bring great meaning and peace to your life, but it is never ultimately about you in isolation from others.

The question at hand is, How best will I serve others?

How will I put my love into action?

REFLECTION

▶ *How should I be serving others?*

▶ *Do I see a consistent pattern or theme to my discomfort and anxiety? What might God be saying to me through this?*

The principle runs through all life from top to bottom. Give up yourself, and you will find your real self. Lose your life and you will save it. Submit to death, death of your ambitions and favorite wishes every day and the death of your whole body in the end: submit with every fiber of your being, and you will find eternal life. Keep back nothing. Nothing that you have not given away will be really yours. Nothing in you that has not died will ever be raised from the dead. Look for yourself, and you will find in the long run only hatred, loneliness, despair, rage, ruin, and decay. But look for Christ and you will find him, and with him everything else thrown in.

—C.S. LEWIS

SURRENDER ALL TO MARY

BOBBY

I am a mama's boy. I have always loved my mother and wanted to make her proud. I was blessed with a dad I could always rely on and wrestle with whenever he got home from work, but there's just something about mom that made it easy for me to open up to her about personal struggles, share my heart, and find peace lying next to her heart.

As a mama's boy, I have also always had a love for Mary, the Mother of Christ. Paintings, stained glass, and statues honoring Our Lady have surrounded me from my youth, and they fill my home today. If devotion to Mary seems excessive to you, don't fear. We can never be afraid of loving too much; as St. Maximilian Kolbe said, we can never love her more than Jesus did.

As an advocate for our journey and decision making, I do not think that we can find a more powerful intercessor than Mary. Called the Seat of Wisdom, Star of the Sea, and Terror of Demons (among many other awesome titles), she has guided the Church throughout the centuries and has guided so many saints seeking to bring Christ to the world. In growing spiritually closer to Mary, I found myself more aligned to the will of God and more at peace in the uncertainty of life itself.

The Reed of God, by Caryll Houselander, an English mystic and writer, had a profound impact on my journey. The book still sits on my bedside table today. Chock-full of simple yet accessible wisdom, Houselander's book details how Mary allowed herself to be but an instrument in the hand of God the artist, and the world was transformed because of her docility. God's will was not a threat to Mary's freedom but rather the fullness of what freedom could be. Shortly after reading this book, I did the thirty-three-day Marian consecration, a formal method of meditating on the role of Mary in salvation history and then offering yourself through her to Christ. On the other side of the country, Jackie did that same consecration to Mary in the same year, though our stories would not intermingle for a few more years. Mary and the Lord had more work to do.

Mary has been walking alongside me for a long time now, and she wants to accompany you as well. I pray that you come to appreciate and know Mary as a bold, confident, and steadfast guide for your road ahead.

Our Lady said yes to God's plan for her life, and the world was forever changed.

What will you say?

————

Mary knew well about making a life-changing decision. When the angel came to her to announce her favor with God, she followed up her questions with an emphatic yes, her *fiat:* "Let it be to me according to your word" (Luke 1:38). Mary did not understand all the "hows" of her future, but she had a radical trust in the goodness of God and knew he would not abandon her on the journey ahead.

As Catholics, we have a special ally on our side to whom we can run and beg for additional guidance on our way. Higher than all the angels and chief among the holy men and women experiencing the glory of heaven is Mary, the Queen of Heaven, the Seat of Wisdom, the Mother of God, and our own spiritual mother.

Mary was assumed body and soul into the grace of heaven—she is therefore alive and well. Like any good mother, she respects our freedom but will lavish the graces of God upon all who dare to ask.

During her life after the Annunciation, Mary set off "in haste" through the hill country to visit her cousin Elizabeth. A pregnant woman traveling through a hill country should be inspiration enough, let alone one traveling "in haste." Mary did not waste time agonizing over her decisions; she *acted.* When the providential time of the Lord came, *she moved.*

Reflecting on Mary's example, where in your life do you need to trust radically? What decision are you agonizing over, feeling that it is all up to you? How is God calling you to act?

In Mary we have a fellow sister in our humanity and a perfect role model of boldness and trust in God. She is advocating for us in this life and wishes more than anything for us to experience the fullness of life and the freedom found only in God. Consider this title of Mary: Star of the Sea. In times of trial or stormy seas, we can rest in the safe harbor of her mantle and follow her direction toward the next destination.

Consider consecrating yourself to Jesus through Mary, a practice recommended by St. Louis de Montfort, St. Maximilian Kolbe, and St. John Paul II. Fr. Michael Gaitley included a modern format of this prayer in his book *33 Days to Morning Glory* that is extremely easy to understand and use. This act of entrustment formally places one under the protection of Our Lady and hands over all one's goods, one's finances, and one's decisions and outcomes into her hands. Mary takes all of our offerings and purifies them and hands them to Christ himself. The fastest road to the heart of Christ is through his own mother!

As St. John Paul II asserted, "This woman of faith, Mary of Nazareth, the Mother of God, has been given to us as a model in our pilgrimage of faith. From Mary, we learn to surrender to God's will in all things. From Mary, we learn to trust even when all hope seems gone. From Mary, we learn to love Christ, her Son and the Son of God."[4] As you move toward the next step of your journey, look to Mary as a steadfast guide and inspirational example of radical trust in God's faithfulness.

Step out as Mary did ... and be not afraid!

---

4   John Paul II, Homily (October 6, 1979), vatican.va/.

REFLECTION

▶ *What is your relationship to Mary like?*

▶ *Have you ever entrusted Mary with significant parts of your journey?*

▶ *If so, what has been the result?*

HAIL, HOLY QUEEN

———————

Hail, Holy Queen, Mother of mercy,
our life, our sweetness, and our hope.
To thee do we cry,
poor banished children of Eve;
to thee do we send up our sighs,
mourning and weeping
in this valley of tears.
Turn, then, most gracious advocate,
thine eyes of mercy toward us,
and after this, our exile, show unto us
the blessed fruit of thy womb, Jesus.
O clement, O loving, O sweet Virgin Mary.

EPILOGUE

*Take heart young people! Christ is calling
you and the world awaits you!*[1]

—ST. JOHN PAUL II

Søren Kierkegaard, a Danish philosopher of the nineteenth century, lived during a time of great scientific advancement. Many people tried to apply the same scientific and empirical formulas to matters of faith. Whether attempting to arrive at certainty in God or to rule God out with certainty, they approached the riddle of God as if he were a mathematical enigma.

Kierkegaard, however, asserted that a life lived in God is not a problem to be solved but a mystery to be lived. We will never have true certainty on matters of faith, the mysteries of God, or even how all of our decisions will pan out. That is part of the adventure and mystery of God's desire for us to be active agents in our own stories.

Kierkegaard penned this poignant prayer:

Teach me, O God, not to torture myself, not to make a martyr out of myself through stifling reflection, but rather teach me to breathe deeply in faith.[2]

Breathe deeply in faith.

1   John Paul II, *The Meaning of Vocation* (Princeton, NJ: Scepter, 1997), 23.
2   Søren Kierkegaard, *The Prayers of Kierkegaard,* ed. Perry D. LeFevre (Chicago: University of Chicago Press, 1956).

Remember that God sees our identity first. Before anything we do or achieve, we are beloved. Our God calls us forth from eternity and loves us as unique, unrepeatable individuals; he calls us by name (see John 10:3). He is a Trinitarian God: a Father who loves us, a Son who walks alongside us, and a Holy Spirit who breathes courage and peace into us. Being made for community, we must put what we are into action, however big or small. We all have something to contribute to the body of Christ.

Sometimes life throws curveballs at us. You may have chosen right or maybe you chose wrong, but take heart that you did the process right. Take what you know now and begin again. Discernment is not a one-time thing. For a Christian, listening to the voice of God and discerning his will is a way of life that does not end. Now you know the process, continue to employ this method, and you will continue to walk in God's will.

Be where you are. Listen to the voice of God. Action will open up the path ahead. Take a step forward, and God will handle the rest.

Pray, decide, and don't worry!

APPENDIX

RECOMMENDED WAYS OF PRAYER AND GROWING IN FAITH

When asked by a journalist about how many ways there are to find God, the future Pope Benedict XVI asserted, "As many as there are people." Our journey in discovering the Lord's will is an intensely personal one. Yet we cannot get around the fact that prayer is not an optional detail in the journey. We all need to pray to best hear the voice of the Lord.

If you are looking for some quick tips to get started, consider the following:

ADORATION
Jesus has given us his very Body and Blood, Soul and Divinity in the host of the Eucharist. You can pray in your room, in nature, or even in your car, but there is no substitute for being before the Eucharist and the presence of Christ himself. Find a church in your area that has twenty-four-hour Adoration. Start with fifteen minutes of prayer and then build up to longer periods of time.

THE MASS
The Mass is the source and summit of our Faith. Try to get to Mass early and stay for a few minutes of gratitude at the end. Reflect on the readings ahead of time. To come close to the heart of Christ, participate in the Mass as often as you can. Find a daily Mass to attend during the week.

CONFESSION

Christ gives his disciples the ability to loose and bind sins (see Matthew 18:18), and he urges us to confess our sins to one another (see James 5:16). There is power in the sacrament of Reconciliation to reconcile us back into the right relationship with God. The priest sits *in persona Christi,* which means that it is not Fr. So-and-So sitting in front of you but Christ himself hearing your sins and wiping them clean. Consider going once a month if you do not go regularly.

FASTING

Fasting without God's involvement is simply dieting. Fasting is meant to put us back in touch with our hunger and dependency upon God. In the Gospels, Christ asserts that certain demons cannot be overcome without fasting accompanying prayer (see Mark 9:29).

ALMSGIVING

When we detach from our wealth, we learn to unmake an idol of money. God has given us everything; do we trust him with even our finances? Tithing means "a tenth," or giving ten percent of our wealth.

SILENCE

As covered in Chapter 3, simply praying in silence is a profound sign of intimacy before the Lord.

THE ROSARY

St. John Paul II considered the Rosary as pondering the mysteries of Christ with Mary by his side; it was a daily meeting with her he never neglected. Start by praying one decade with your specific intention in mind. Check out Matt Fradd's *Pocket Guide to the Rosary,* which will encourage and inspire you to make this essential Catholic prayer a habit.

QUICK PRAYERS

▶ *Come, Holy Spirit.* Say this prayer in your heart whenever you are stressed, in need of clarity, or trying to find the right words to say.

▶ *Lord Jesus, Son of God, have mercy on me, a sinner.* The "Jesus prayer" is a simple prayer meant to be repeated.

RECOMMENDED RESOURCES

The following books are excellent resources for further wisdom and guidance.

PRAYER AND KNOWLEDGE OF SELF

▶ *Prayer for Beginners* – Dr. Peter Kreeft

▶ *Abandonment to Divine Providence (The Sacrament of the Present Moment)* – Jean-Pierre de Caussade

▶ *The Soul of the Apostolate* – Jean-Baptiste Chautard

▶ *The Temperament God Gave You: The Classic Key to Knowing Yourself, Getting Along with Others, and Growing Closer to the Lord* – Art and Laraine Bennett

▶ *The War of Art* – Steven Pressfield

▶ *The Power of Agency: The 7 Principles to Conquer Obstacles, Make Effective Decisions, and Create a Life on Your Own Terms* – Dr. Paul Napper and Dr. Anthony Rao

VIRTUOUS AND CHASTE LIVING

▶ *Men, Women and the Mystery of Love: Practical Insights from John Paul II's* Love and Responsibility – Dr. Edward Sri

▶ *Delivered: True Stories of Men and Women Who Turned from Porn to Purity* – Matt Fradd

▶ *Emotional Virtue: A Guide to Drama-Free Relationships* – Sarah Swafford

▶ *Cleansed: A Catholic Guide to Freedom from Porn* – Marcel LeJeune

▶ *Back to Virtue* – Dr. Peter Kreeft

▶ *How to Find Your Soulmate Without Losing Your Soul: 21 Secrets for Women* – Jason and Crystalina Evert

▶ *Made for Love: Same-Sex Attractions and the Catholic Church* – Fr. Michael Schmitz

IGNATIAN DISCERNMENT AND SPIRITUALITY

▶ *God's Voice Within: The Ignatian Way to Discover God's Will* – Fr. Mark E. Thibodeaux, SJ

▶ *Weeds Among the Wheat* – Fr. Thomas H. Green, SJ

▶ *When the Well Runs Dry: Prayer Beyond the Beginnings* – Fr. Thomas H. Green, SJ

▶ *The Discernment of Spirits: An Ignatian Guide for Everyday Living* – Fr. Timothy M. Gallagher, OMV

▶ *Discerning the Will of God: The Ignatian Guide to Christian Decision Making* – Fr. Timothy M. Gallagher, OMV

VOCATION: MARRIAGE OR PRIESTHOOD AND RELIGIOUS LIFE

▶ *Three to Get Married* – Ven. Fulton J. Sheen

▶ *Forever: A Catholic Devotional for Your Marriage* – Jackie Francois Angel and Bobby Angel

▶ *To Save a Thousand Souls: A Guide for Discerning a Vocation to Diocesan Priesthood* – Fr. Brett A. Brannen

▶ *The Priest Is Not His Own* – Ven. Fulton J. Sheen

▶ *Discerning Religious Life* – Sr. Clare Matthiass, CFR

MARY

▶ *33 Days to Morning Glory: A Do-It-Yourself Retreat in Preparation for Marian Consecration* – Fr. Michael E. Gaitley, MIC

▶ *True Devotion to Mary* – St. Louis de Montfort

▶ *The Reed of God* – Caryll Houselander

▶ *The World's First Love* – Ven. Fulton J. Sheen

ACKNOWLEDGMENTS

Thank you to all the people at Ascension who supported this project from the beginning, especially our project manager, Andrew Lanchoney, who kept the book on track and kept us laughing along the way.

Thank you to all the priests, spiritual directors, formators, and mentors who guided our journeys along the way.

Thank you to all our families and friends. Your love, patience, and support during this project helped bring this book to fruition.

Lastly, thank you to Almighty God for blessing us with the adventure of our lives.

To Christ be the glory, forever and ever! Amen.

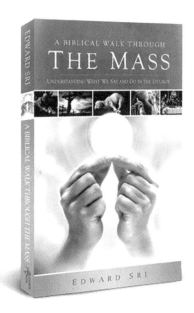

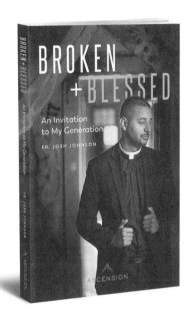